Aesthetic
COLORING
BOOK

Inspired Life Creative

MW01602942

© 2021, Inspired Life Creative
All Rights Reserved.

No part of this book may be reproduced in any form or
by any electronic or mechanical means, including
information storage and retrieval systems, without
explicit permission in writing from the publisher.

ISBN: 9798527443349

Published by Inspired Life Creative

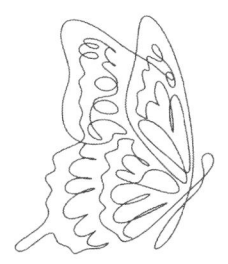

THIS COLORING BOOK
BELONGS TO:

_____

_____

_____

_____

_____

COLOR TEST PAGE

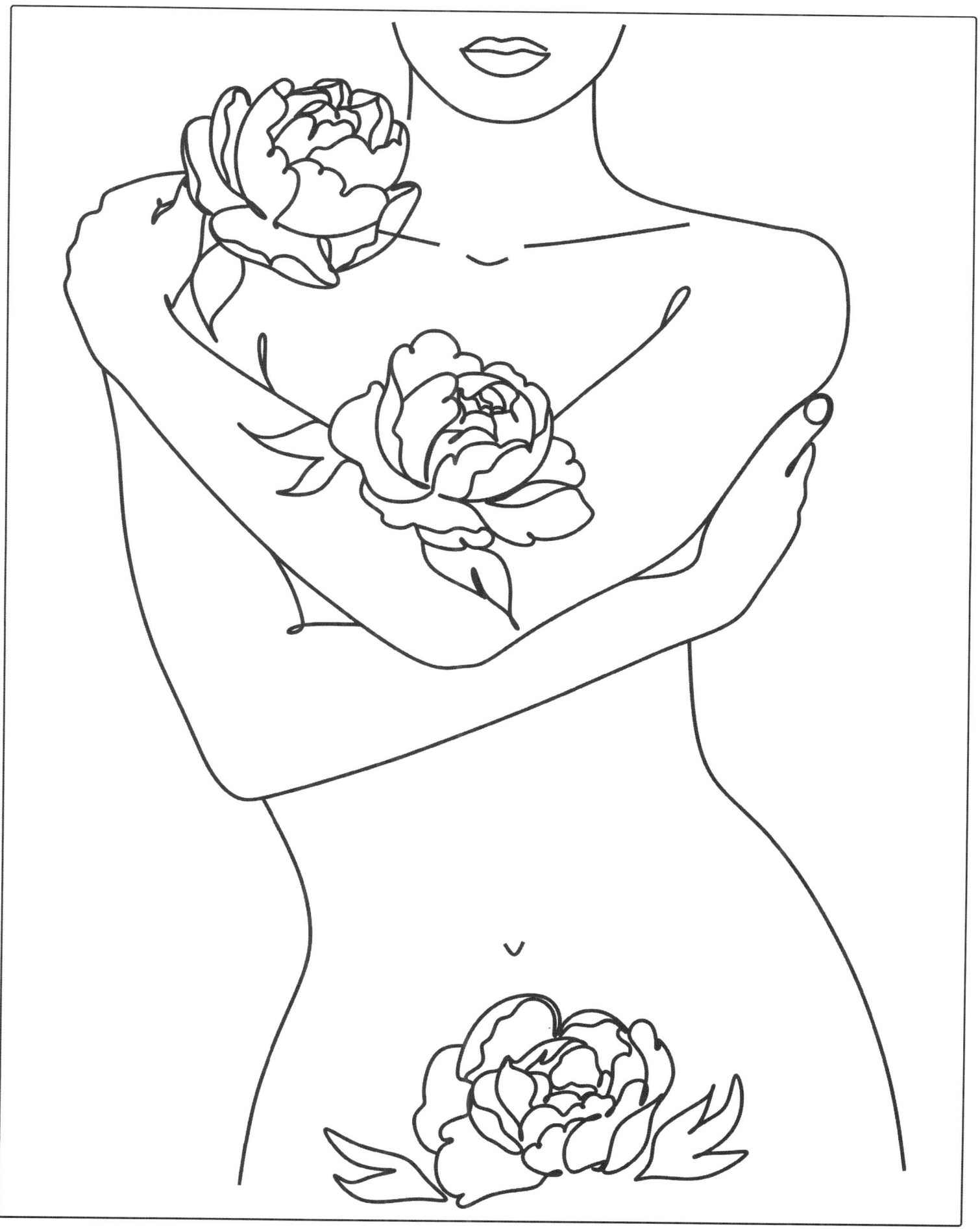

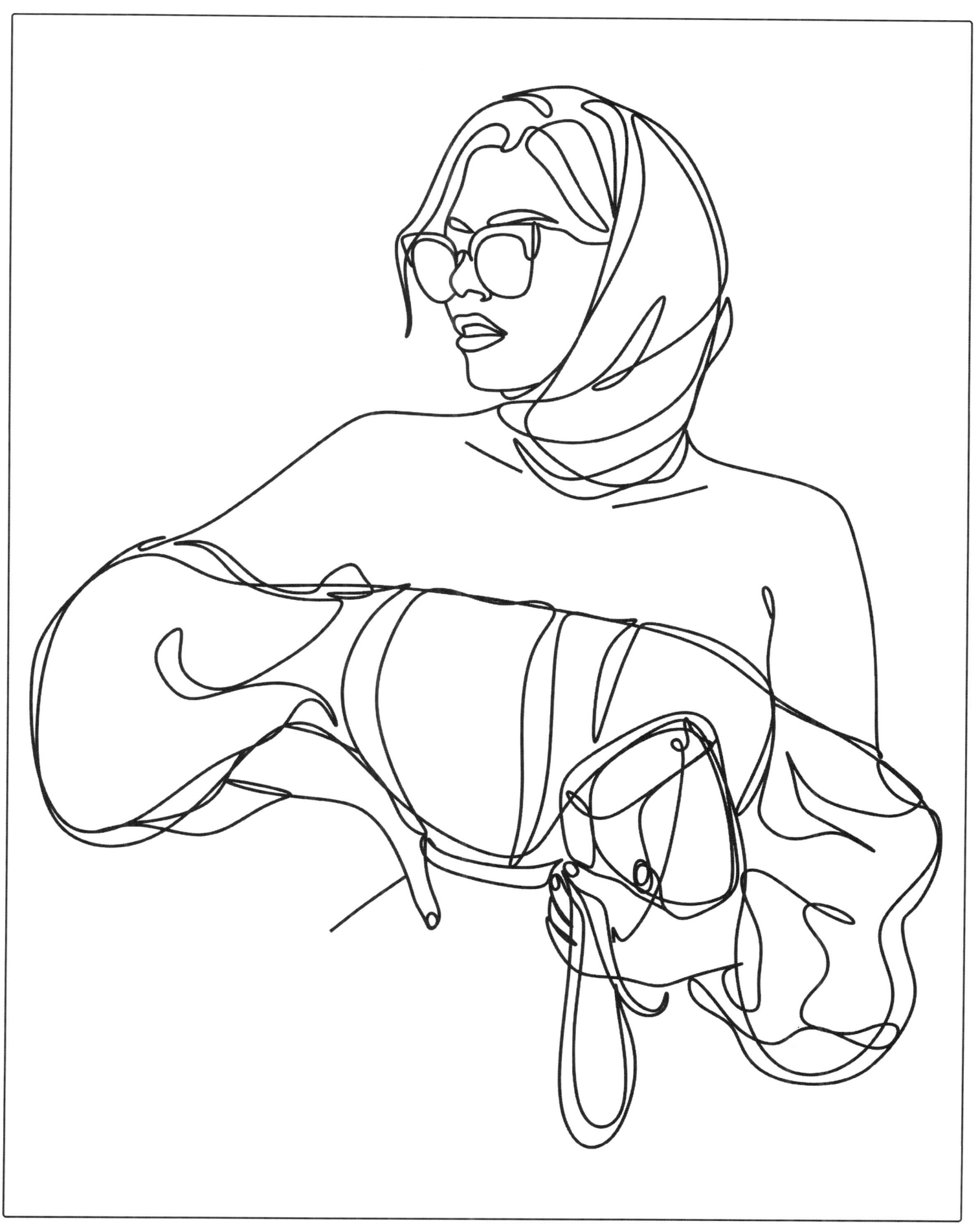

Made in the USA
Middletown, DE
08 February 2022

60786206R00071